SATURDAYS AT
HARLEM  GROWN

How One Big Idea Transformed a Neighborhood

To Nana and Pop: Greta and Frank Wilkins; Mom and Dad: Virginia and Harold Hillery; my wife, Mary, and children, Toni, Zachary, and Raechel; and my granddaughters, Zaria and Zoe.

I also gratefully acknowledge the constant help and support of my partner in change, Executive Director Nicole Engel; Kristen Rocha Aldrich for helping me write this; the hardworking staff at Harlem Grown; the inspiration and original children: Nevaeh Seeley, Epiphany Adams, Kadiatu and Nanteen Ba, Aissatou and Gorgui Seck, and Donovan Burgos; and all the amazing children of Harlem who make our work so meaningful.

—T. H.

To city dwellers everywhere longing for a patch of green and a sense of community.

—J. H.

The author's portion of proceeds from this book are being paid directly to Harlem Grown, Inc. For more information about Harlem Grown, please visit harlemgrown.org.

SIMON & SCHUSTER BOOKS FOR YOUNG READERS
An imprint of Simon & Schuster Children's Publishing Division
1230 Avenue of the Americas, New York, New York 10020

Text © 2024 by Harlem Grown, Inc.
Illustration © 2024 by Jessie Hartland
Book design by Lucy Ruth Cummins

Simon & Schuster: Celebrating 100 Years of Publishing in 2024. For information about special discounts for bulk purchases, please contact
Simon & Schuster Special Sales at 1-866-506-1949 or business@simonandschuster.com.

The Simon & Schuster Speakers Bureau can bring authors to your live event.
For more information or to book an event, contact the Simon & Schuster Speakers Bureau at 1-866-248-3049 or visit our website at www.simonspeakers.com.

The text for this book was set in Blocky Fill. The illustrations for this book were rendered in gouache.
Manufactured in China · 0224 SCP · First Edition
2 4 6 8 10 9 7 5 3 1

Library of Congress Cataloging-in-Publication Data
Names: Hillery, Tony, author. | Hartland, Jessie, illustrator.
Title: Saturdays at Harlem Grown / Tony Hillery ; illustrated by Jessie Hartland.
Description: First edition. | New York : Simon & Schuster Books for Young Readers, 2024. | "A Paula Wiseman Book." | Audience: Ages 4–8. | Audience: Grades 2–3. |
Summary: It is harvest time at the revitalized urban community farm called Harlem Grown.
Identifiers: LCCN 2023031907 (print) | LCCN 2023031908 (ebook) | ISBN 9781665929783 (hardcover) | ISBN 9781665929790 (ebook)
Subjects: CYAC: Community gardens—Fiction. | Harlem (New York, N.Y.)—Fiction. | LCGFT: Picture books.
Classification: LCC PZ7.1.H5638 Sat 2024 (print) | LCC PZ7.1.H5638 (ebook) | DDC [E]—dc23
LC record available at https://lccn.loc.gov/2023031907
LC ebook record available at https://lccn.loc.gov/2023031908

SATURDAYS AT HARLEM GROWN

How One Big Idea Transformed a Neighborhood

WRITTEN BY TONY HILLERY

ILLUSTRATED BY JESSIE HARTLAND

A Paula Wiseman Book · Simon & Schuster Books for Young Readers · New York London Toronto Sydney New Delhi

Once, in a big city called New York, in a

bustling neighborhood called Harlem, there was a farm.

Nevaeh visited the farm every Saturday with her family.

It was lush with fruits,
vegetables, herbs, and flowers.
She helped build it with Mr. Tony.

But it hadn't always been a farm!
Not so very long ago, it was a sad,
empty, trash-filled lot.

Mr. Tony, who worked at PS 175 across the street,

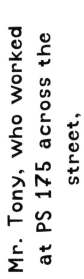

and Nevaeh, a young student at the school, had an idea.

They cleared away all the trash.

They brought in good soil.

And they planted a garden.

The garden was so beautiful in spring, summer, and fall.

And very SAD in the winter.

So on snowy days, Nevaeh and Mr. Tony thought about what to plant in the spring.

Finally, spring arrived.

Mr. Tony asked Nevaeh,

"How on earth can we do all this work ourselves?"

They had an idea.

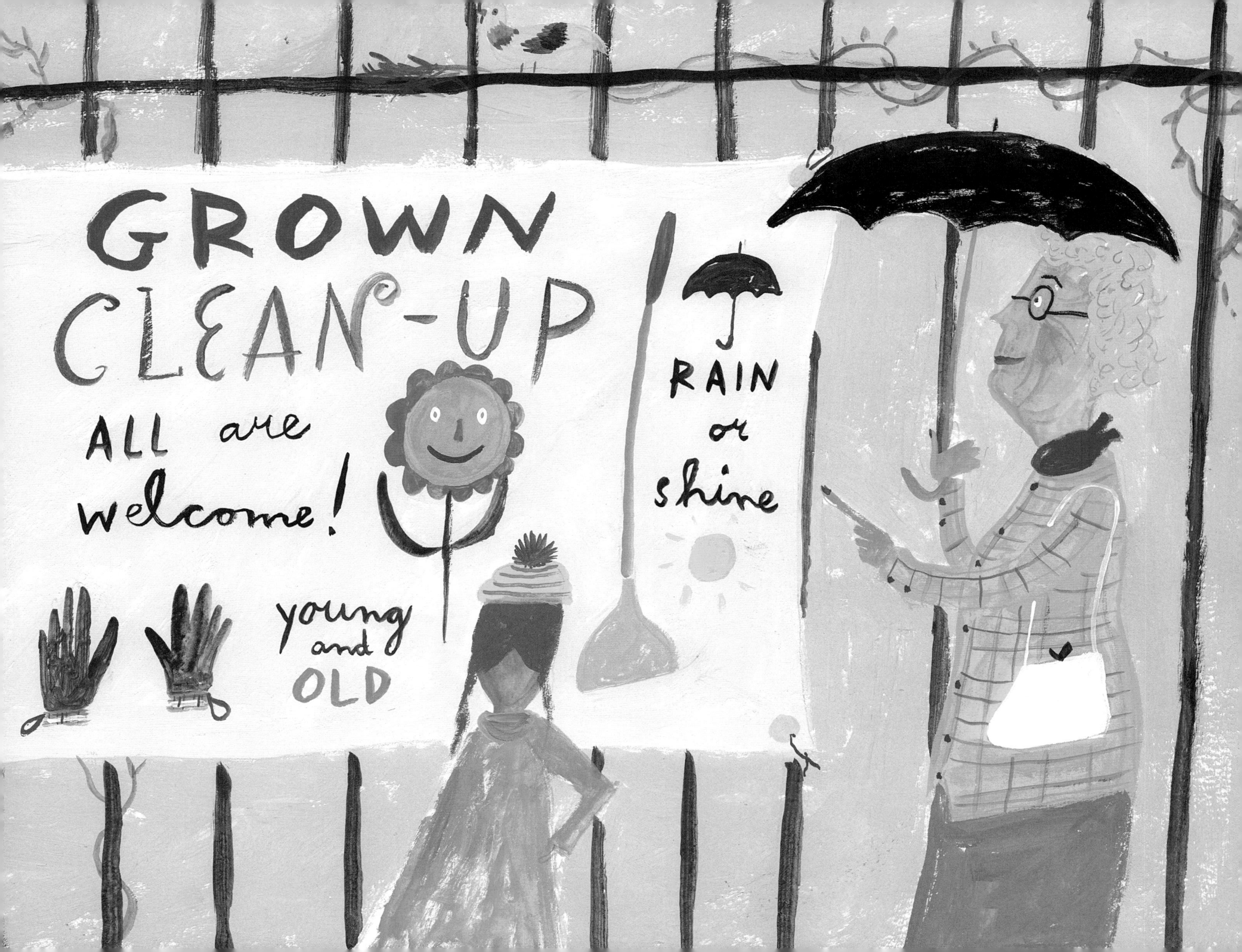
GROWN CLEAN-UP
ALL are welcome!
young and OLD
RAIN or shine

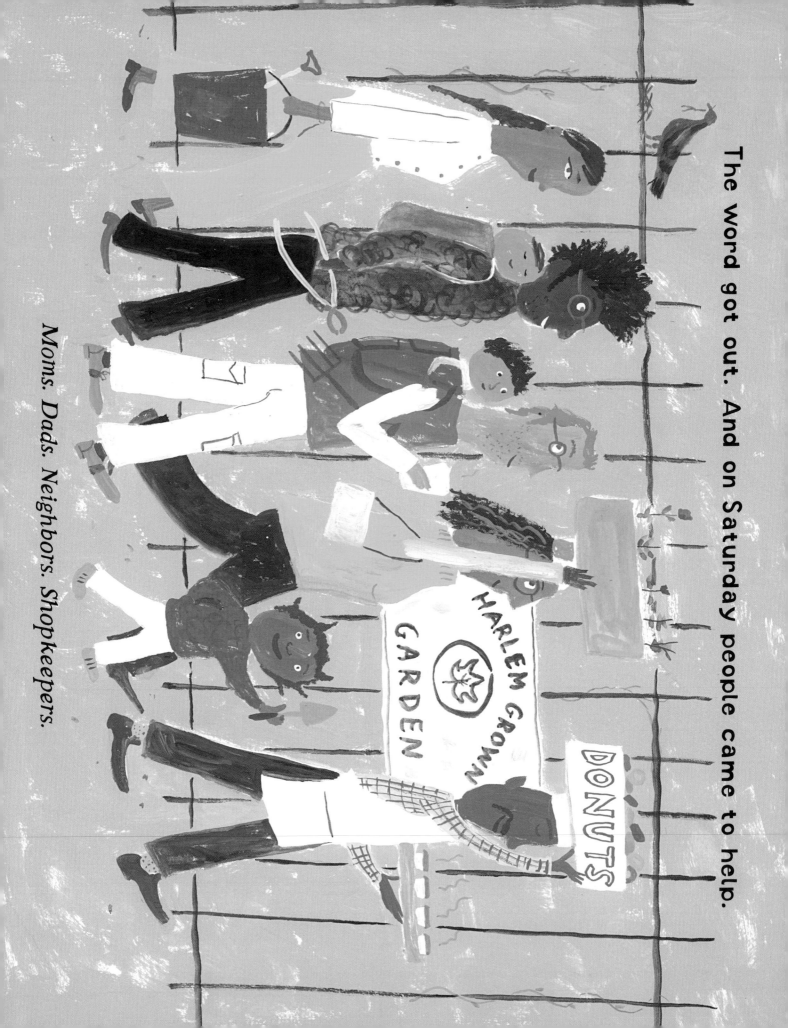

The word got out. And on Saturday people came to help.

Moms. Dads. Neighbors. Shopkeepers.

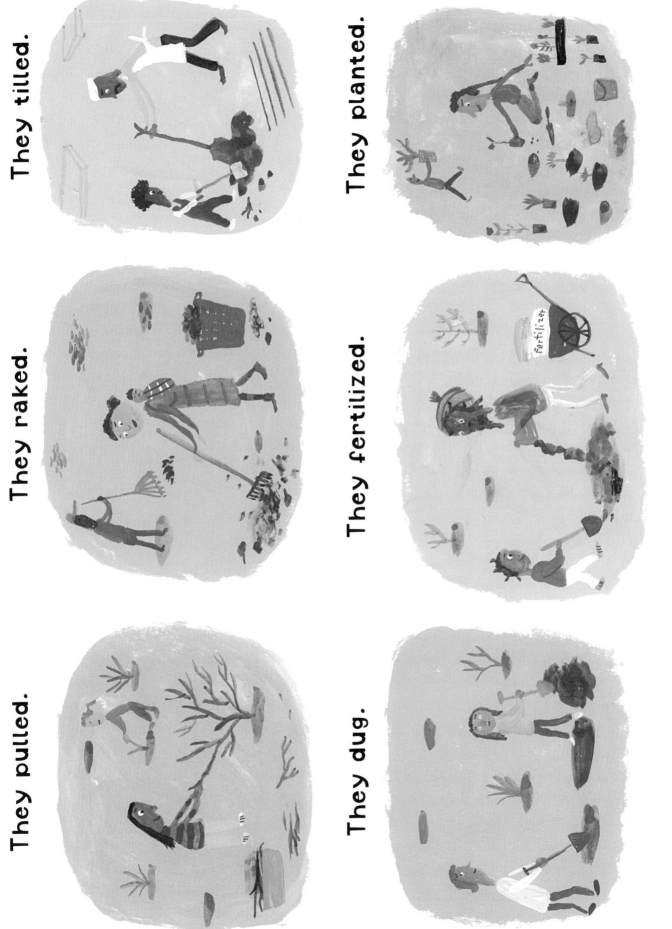

They tilled.

They raked.

They pulled.

They planted.

They fertilized.

They dug.

Soon there were clean garden beds. Fresh soil. And plenty of room to grow.

And the next Saturday

they came again.

Friends.

Grandparents.

Neighbors.

Teenagers.

Even more people than

the week before.

Soon there were more

clean garden beds.

Fresh patches of dirt.

And tools to help.

A shovel for digging.

A rake for leveling.

A hand hoe for weeding.

And a watering can to help

the seeds grow.

HARLEM GROWN GARDEN

HARLEM GROWN GARDEN

CHICKENS

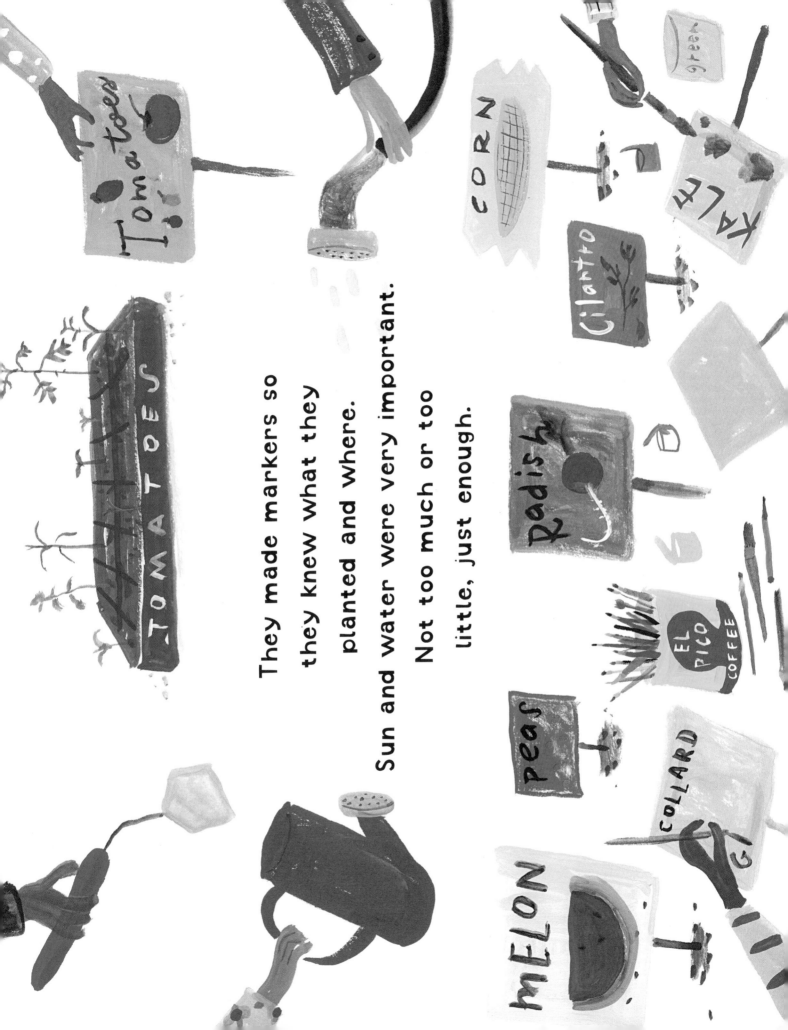

They made markers so
they knew what they
planted and where.
Sun and water were very important.
Not too much or too
little, just enough.

Day by day they watched and waited. And waited. And waited.

And while they waited for the seeds to sprout,
Nevaeh and Mr. Tony taught the community
about healthy eating with what they were growing,

and they shared recipes to make
at home with produce from the farm.

They also taught the community how to help save our Earth through composting and recycling.

They even built a library where people could read books about urban farming and cooking.

It seemed to take forever. Until one day, a sprout appeared.

Bit by bit, it grew.

Big.

Bigger and bigger.

Biggest.

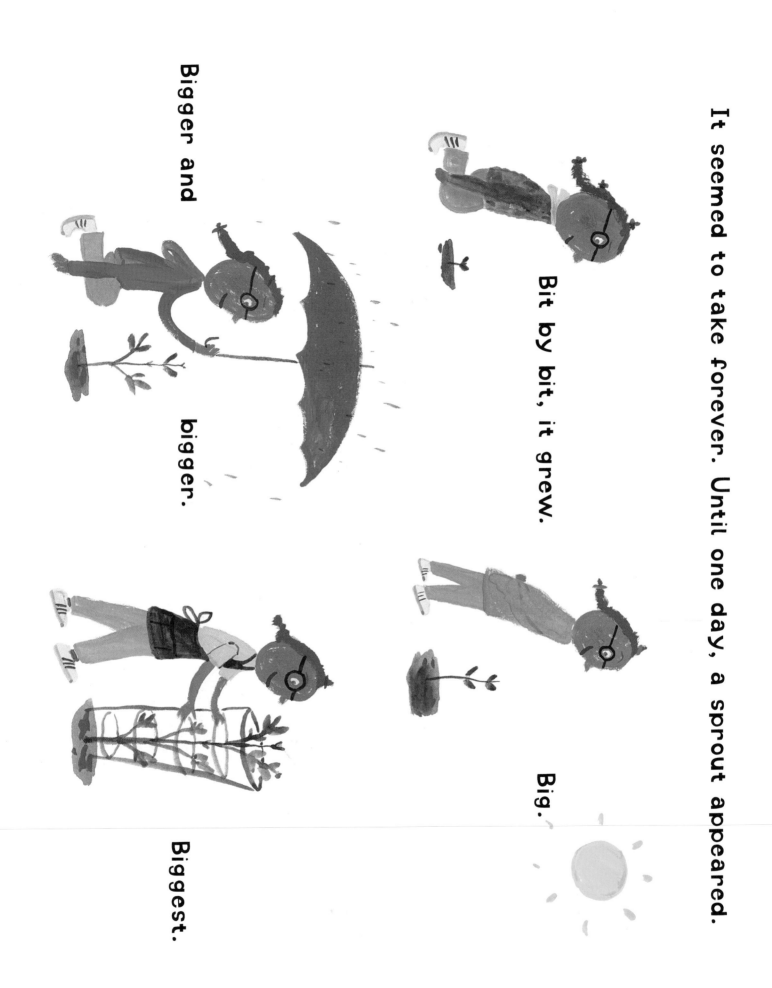

Bright red peppers.

Yellow corn. Juicy tomatoes.

Mint. Basil. Cilantro.

HARLEM GROWN

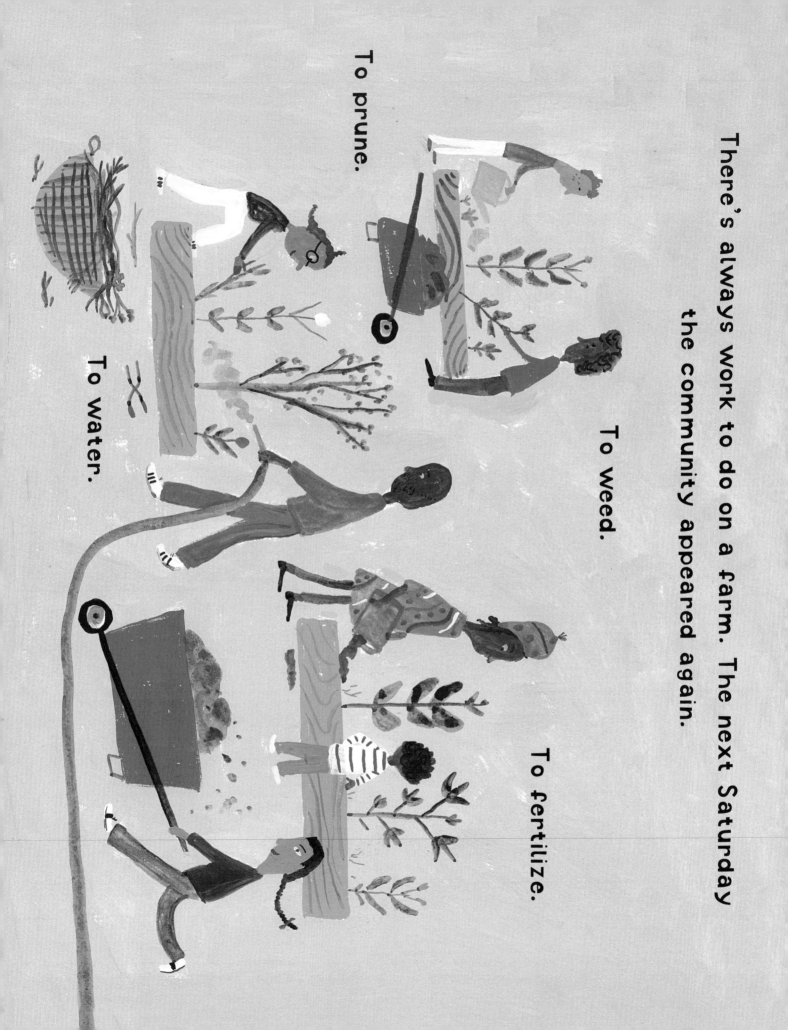

There's always work to do on a farm. The next Saturday the community appeared again.

To prune.

To weed.

To water.

To fertilize.

People came to share their skills.

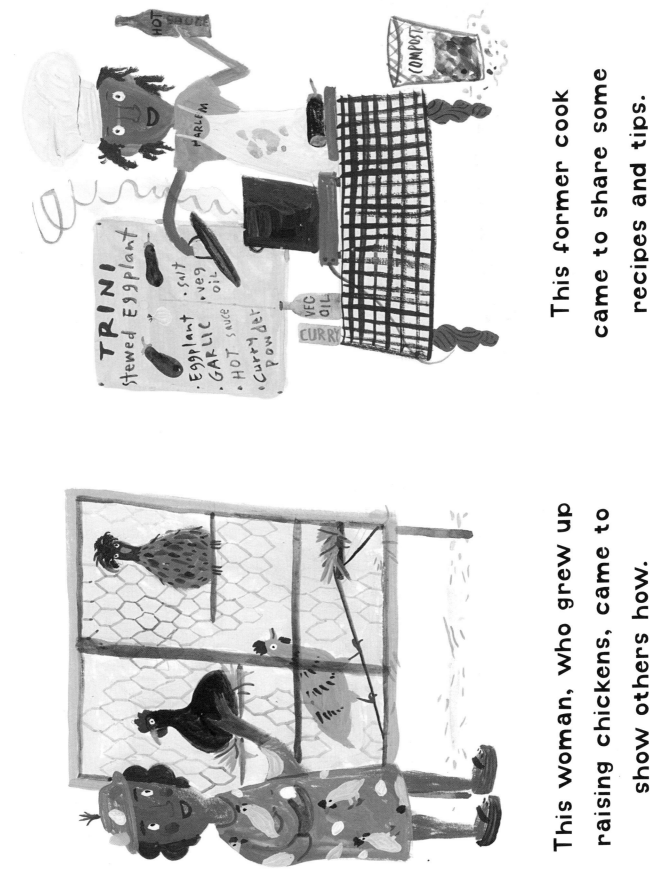

This former cook came to share some recipes and tips.

This woman, who grew up raising chickens, came to show others how.

A carpenter built
new planters.

An author read her book.

A plumber
came to help
build watering
pipes.

An electrician
helped to put
in lighting.

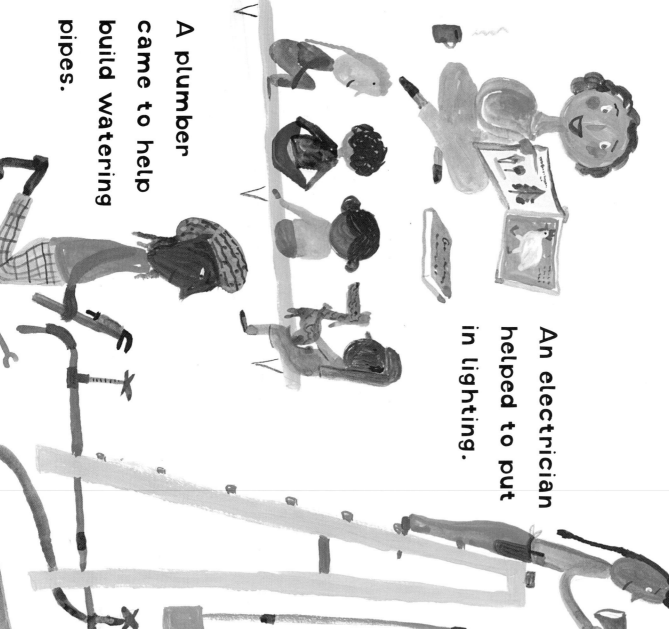

They took home
fresh produce
and flower
arrangements.

And at last, a harvest! "Nevaeh," asked Mr. Tony, "how should we celebrate all our hard work?"

"We need to have a party!" And so they did.

On Saturday the
community came
together again,
and they . . . .

ate homegrown food

and looked at teeny-
tiny things under
microscopes.

Finally, the day of the harvest festival!

Once, in a big city called New York,
in a bustling neighborhood called Harlem,
there was a farm.
Nevaeh wanted to share.
People wanted to help.
They grew a garden.
And together they
grew a community, too.

They learned new recipes and made new friends.

They made birdhouses,

decorated apples,

and said goodbye.

HARLEM GROWN

UNTIL next YEAR!

Dear Reader,

First, I'd like to thank everyone who supported my first book, *Harlem Grown: How One Big Idea Transformed a Neighborhood*. By doing so, you supported the higher education of, and a life-changing experience for, countless children.

In 2011, when I started volunteering at PS 175, I met children who changed *my* life. These children were exactly like my three children: funny, curious, optimistic, and extremely intelligent. Soon after working in the school, I learned about the social determinants of health, which clearly state that these children will have a completely different life experience from my own because of where they live. Forgive me, but we live in the richest city in the world: How can this be?

When I saw the vacant lot across the street from PS 175, I started Harlem Grown—an urban farm where we plant fruits and vegetables, but *grow* healthy children and sustainable communities—and built a bridge from more affluent areas to our garden.

At Harlem Grown, our children are introduced to much more than planting vegetables—they are shown all the possibilities the world has to offer by way of the thousands of volunteers who come to help and share their time with us.

Now our children want to pursue so many career paths, including accounting, engineering, architecture, and medicine, simply by being exposed. These opportunities have changed not only our children but me as well.

After a life of business, you kind of lose sight of what's important. Changing careers at age fifty-one was scary at first, but almost immediately, once I was "Mr. Tony," everything changed.

They say it's never too late to change, but be careful, as that change just might lead to your own Harlem Grown.

PHOTO BY TAU BATTICE

Sincerely,

Tony Hillery

Founder and Director of Harlem Grown

Here are our farms, now fourteen strong:

Farm Sites
127th Street Farm and Greenhouse
127th Street Learning Annex
131st Street Farm
134th Street Farm
134th Street Greenhouse
134th Street Pollinator Lot
134th Street Mushroom Chamber
Riverton Houses Biodome
139th Street Freight Farm

Partner Schools
PS 125
PS 154
PS 197
St. HOPE Leadership Academy
Thurgood Marshall Academy Lower School

START AN URBAN SCHOOL COMMUNITY GARDEN

STEP 1: Gather your community. Organize a garden committee, including your principal, parent coordinator, and others.

STEP 2: Pick and secure a site, and make a plan. Identify an unused lot or empty space at school or in your neighborhood. Secure funding and sponsorships.

STEP 3: Choose your plants. Plan short- and long-term crops. Find and use seasonal and regional crops.

STEP 4: Begin planting, and connect it to academics to enhance support. Start seedlings in unused household containers, cans, or milk cartons. Build raised beds with non-pressurized lumber or large food containers.

STEP 5: Visit your garden every day—weed, water, and check on the plants.

STEP 6: Harvest and share—celebrate your garden and volunteers. Host Earth Day events, monthly family-friendly garden-based activities, or potluck meals with garden-grown produce.

STEP 7: Encourage composting to ensure nutrient-rich soil.

STEP 8: Winterize your garden by planting winter-hardy crops. Build cold frames to go over each bed. Use PVC piping to make hoops over the beds, and cover them with plastic sheeting.

ENJOY YOUR HARVEST AND MAKE VEGETABLE SOUP

All kinds of produce can be used to make vegetable soup. You can cook with carrots, celery, potatoes, tomatoes, zucchini, corn, beans, onions, garlic, or any other fresh vegetables from your garden.

INGREDIENTS

1 tablespoon olive oil
1 yellow onion, sliced
1 clove garlic, chopped
3 medium-sized carrots, chopped
2 stalks celery, chopped

7 cups broth or water
5 tomatoes, chopped
1 cup additional fresh vegetables from your garden, chopped

1 tablespoon salt
Black pepper, oregano, and basil to taste
1 tablespoon parsley, chopped

DIRECTIONS

1. With an adult helper, heat the olive oil in a pot, and sauté the onion in the oil until tender but not browned.
2. Add the garlic, and cook for one minute until softened but not browned.
3. Add the carrots and celery, and cook for four minutes or until soft.
4. Add the broth or water and the tomatoes.
5. Stir in the additional vegetables.
6. Cook over medium heat until all the vegetables are soft.
7. Add the salt and the other spices of choice to taste.
8. Sprinkle with the parsley. Serve hot.

ADDITIONAL RESOURCES

FOR ALL AGES:

Web
harlemgrown.org
jmgkids.us
kidsgardening.org
njaes.rutgers.edu/home-lawn-garden/gardening-with-youth.php

Books

Gibbons, Gail. *From Seed to Plant*. New York: Holiday House, 1991.
Gibbons, Gail. *The Vegetables We Eat: New and Updated*. New York: Holiday House, 2024.
Krezel, Cindy. *Kids' Container Gardening: Year-Round Projects for Inside and Out*. Chicago: Chicago Review Press, 2010.
Lerner, Carol. *My Backyard Garden*. New York: William Morrow & Co, 1998.
Tornio, Stacy. *Project Garden: A Month-by-Month Guide to Planting, Growing, and Enjoying ALL Your Backyard Has to Offer*.
  Avon, MA: Adams Media, 2012.

FOR ADULTS:

Web
For an extensive list of resources about starting a community, urban, or school garden, visit
  n2ncentre.com//education-support/parent-resources

For information about starting a school garden, visit slowfoodusa.org/school-gardens/grants-garden-guide *and*
  brightbites.ca/wp-content/uploads/seeds-for-success-final.pdf

For information about starting a garden in containers in your home, school, or neighborhood, visit eatright.org

Books

Bucklin-Sporer, Arden, and Rachel Kathleen Pringle. *How to Grow a School Garden: A Complete Guide for Parents and Teachers*. Portland, OR: Timber Press, 2010.
Carpenter, Novella. *Farm City: The Education of an Urban Farmer*. New York: Penguin Press, 2009.
Carpenter, Novella, and Willow Rosenthal. *The Essential Urban Farmer*. New York: Penguin Books, 2011.
Ragan, Jill. *The Tiny but Mighty Farm: Cultivating High Yields, Community, and Self-Sufficiency from a Home Farm*.
  Beverly, MA: Cool Springs Press, 2023.